A Pocket Guide to

HAWAI'I'S
UNDERWATER PARADISE

TEXT AND PHOTOGRAPHS
BY JOHN P. HOOVER

ADDITIONAL PHOTOGRAPHS
BY DAVID R. SCHRICHTE

MUTUAL PUBLISHING

CONTENTS

6 ROCKY SHORES

22 CORAL REEFS

44 CAVES

62 THE SAND

72 COLORS

Copyright © 1997
by John P. Hoover

No part of this book may be
reproduced in any form or by
any electronic or mechanical
means, including information
storage and retrieval devices or
systems, without prior written
permission from the publisher,
except that brief passages may
be quoted for reviews.

All rights reserved
Library of Congress Catalog Card
Number: 97-70284

Design by Angela Wu-Ki

First Printing June 1997
Second Printing, October 1999
Third Printing, July 2001
Fourth Printing, January 2003
Fifth Printing, June 2004
Sixth Printing, June 2005
6 7 8 9

ISBN 1-56647-151-6

Mutual Publishing
1215 Center Street, Suite 210
Honolulu, Hawaii 96816
Telephone (808) 732-1709
Fax (808) 734-4094
e-mail: mutual@mutualpublishing.com
www.mutualpublishing.com

Printed in Taiwan

MUTUAL
PUBLISHING

Introduction

Underwater, Hawai'i is a vast mountain range sprawling 1,500 miles from the Big Island of Hawai'i in the south to Kure Atoll in the north. Most of this range exists in perpetual darkness, deep and cold, its topography and inhabitants only sketchily known. Only toward the tops of the highest seamounts does light begin to glimmer and the temperature start to rise. Some, reaching almost to the surface, become banks, reefs and shoals; the very highest become green islands. The tops of these submarine peaks, underwater and above, are fertile oases in an oceanic desert. In contrast to the gloomy deep, the water here is warm and bright sunlight dances on the sea floor. An abundance of plants and corals provide food and shelter for a wealth of fascinating and colorful creatures.

These islands and their surrounding reefs are the most isolated on Earth. Born of volcanic fires, they originally harbored no life. The only plants and animals to settle here, including humans, were extraordinary long-distance travelers. Some drifted as larvae, a very few swam, other hitched rides. All were survivors of a long, treacherous journey. Stranded, so to speak, on these remote oceanic mountain tops, the descendants of this select group thrived and multiplied in their isolated paradise. Over millions of years many changed, becoming uniquely Hawaiian.

When humans arrived here, the abundance of the surrounding seas sustained them. The Hawaiian people were master fishermen and gatherers of seafood, intimate with the habits and cycles of the sea creatures. Still, they knew them mainly as food, tangled in a net or hooked on a line. Only in this century have men and women had the ability to meet, appreciate and photograph these fascinating, often beautiful animals undisturbed in their own element.

Today, anyone with a mask and snorkel can safely explore Hawai'i's shallow reefs at marine parks such as O'ahu's Hanauma Bay, Maui's Molokini Crater or the Big Island's Kealakekua Bay. With scuba gear, the more adventuresome can remain an hour or more underwater, immersed in a world so totally different that all terrestrial cares and concerns simply drop away. This book provides an introduction to Hawai'i's undersea kingdom and the bounty of creatures in it, many occurring nowhere else in the world. Whether a snorkeler, diver or armchair traveler, you will enjoy the undersea paradise that is Hawai'i.

ROCKY SHORES

Much of Hawai'i's shoreline is composed of lava rock, typically forming low cliffs that plunge into the sea. Below, the bottom is often strewn with great boulders, torn from the land by winter surf. On gentler coasts tide pools dot the shore, while further out a shallow, wave-swept platform may drop dramatically, forming underwater cliffs and canyons riddled with holes and ledges. Coral is sparse on such exposed coasts, but algae grows abundantly—food for a mind-boggling number and variety of fishes and other sea creatures.

ZEBRA BLENNY * **pao'o** (Istiblennius zebra)

The **ZEBRA BLENNY** or Jumping Jack (Istiblennius zebra) is a comical little fish with a wide grin and "ears" like a rabbit. It lives in shallow tide pools. When alarmed, it can jump and slither quite a distance over the rocks from one pool to another, somehow knowing its location in advance.

GARGANTUAN BLENNY (Cirripectes obscurus)

The **GARGANTUAN BLENNY** (Cirripectes obscurus) occupies crevices a few feet below the waterline in places where the wave action is always strong. During spawning season, males develop flame-red heads and yellow pectoral fins. Although common, this species is rarely seen due to its habitat. It occurs only in Hawai'i.

HELMET URCHINS * **ha'uke'uke kaupali** (Colobocentrotus atratus)

HELMET URCHINS (Colobocentrotus atratus) cling to lava shores, scraping algae from the rocks. Their dome-like shape dissipates the force of the waves.

The **HUMPBACK COWRY** (Cypraea mauritiana) nestles in rocky holes along exposed coasts. The shape of its shell—wide at the base and humping almost to a point—helps the animal shed the force of pounding surf. In old Hawai'i, its flesh was eaten and the strong shell fashioned into scrapers for grating coconut.

HUMPBACK COWRY * **lehoahi** (Cypraea mauritiana)

FISH STEW

REEF FLATS AT A DEPTH OF 10 TO 20 FEET SUPPORT AN INCREDIBLE VARIETY OF FISH LIFE. MOST ABUNDANT ARE CHUBS AND SURGEONFISHES (OFTEN CALLED TANGS). ALGAE EATERS, THEY HAVE MOUTHS ADAPTED FOR EITHER SCRAPING THE SURFACE OF ROCKS AND DEAD CORAL OR NIBBLING LEAFY SEAWEEDS. MANY SPECIES COEXIST HERE, EACH PROBABLY SPECIALIZING IN A CERTAIN TYPE OF ALGAE.

SURGEONFISHES at Hanauma Bay, O'ahu, photo by D.R. Schrichte

HIGHFIN CHUBS *(Kyphosus cinerascens)* aggregate along an underwater cliff at the entrance to Hanauma Bay, O'ahu. Some call them rudderfishes, from their habit in olden times of hanging around wooden ships in harbors, grazing the algae from the ships' hulls and rudders. Chubs love handouts. They are often first on the scene at fish feeding sites, swarming around snorkelers, sometimes becoming pushy and aggressive.

HIGHFIN CHUBS * **nenue** *(Kyphosus cinerascens)*

Six species of surgeonfishes crowd a reef flat at the outer entrance to Hanauma Bay, O'ahu. Seen here are Yellow Tangs, Achilles Tangs, Whitebar Surgeonfish, Whitespotted Surgeonfish, Convict Tangs, and a Ringtail Surgeonfish.

SURGEONFISHES at Hanauma Bay, photo by D.R.Schrichte

HAWAIIAN SERGEANTS * **mamo** *(Abudefduf abdominalis)*, photo by D.R.Schrichte

HAWAIIAN SERGEANTS *(Abudefduf abdominalis)* seek refuge in a crevice encrusted with scarlet sponge. Females lay their eggs on the bare rock walls of such crevices; males guard them zealously.

MILLETSEED BUTTERFLYFISH *(Chaetodon miliaris)*

MILLETSEED BUTTERFLYFISHES *(Chaetodon miliaris)*

Swarms of **MILLETSEED BUTTERFLYFISHES** *(Chaetodon miliaris)* gorge on Hawaiian Sergeant eggs, their sheer numbers overcoming the guardian parent. These planktivores do not hesitate to take advantage of other food when they can get it. At fish feeding sites they quickly mob snorkelers and divers who offer a handout. These yellow beauties, often called "lemon butterflyfishes," are found only in Hawai'i.

OPPOSITE PAGE:
MILLETSEED BUTTERFLYFISHES * **lau-wiliwili**
(Chaetodon miliaris)

PENNANT BUTTERFLYFISHES *(Heniochus diphreutes)*

Plankton-eating butterflyfishes and damselfishes of several species are plentiful along rocky shores, feeding well off the bottom. Here, **PENNANT BUTTERFLY-FISHES** *(Heniochus diphreutes)* swarm in graceful disarray above surgeonfishes and Hawaiian Sergeant damselfishes at the outer entrance to Hanauma Bay.

Clouds of White and gold **PYRAMID BUTTERFLYFISHES** *(Hemitaurichthys polylepis)* populate a sheer submarine wall at Lehua Rock, near the island of Ni'ihau. With them are Pennant Butterflyfishes and dark Oval Chromises.

PYRAMID BUTTERFLYFISHES
(Hemitaurichthys polylepis)

ACHILLES TANGS * **paku'iku'i** *(Acanthurus achilles)*, photo by D.R. Schrichte

Surgeonfishes are named for the sharp spines or scalpels at the base of the tail. Normally folded into a groove, the scalpels pop out when the fish sideswipes an enemy; they can cut deeply. These territorial **ACHILLES TANGS** *(Acanthurus achilles)* wear bright orange over their scalpels to warn intruders. They spend much of their time chasing other surgeonfishes away from their patch of algae. When agitated, their entire bodies take on a reddish glow.

BLUESPINE UNICORNFISH * **kala** (Naso unicornis)

Instead of scalpels, the **BLUESPINE UNICORNFISH** (Naso unicornis) flaunts razor-sharp blue keels at the base of its tail. An eater of leafy seaweeds, it is common in shallow water. Here, a male, with its long tail streamers, is seen over Cauliflower Coral, one of the few branching corals that can withstand the constant wave action of exposed shallow shores. No one knows the function of the horn.

CONVICT TANGS * **manini** (Acanthurus triostegus)

CONVICT TANGS (Acanthurus triostegus) are marked with six black bars, the convict's stripes. Called *manini* in Hawaiian, they are among the Islands' best-known fishes. Browsing the reef in dense schools, hundreds of *manini* can sweep into Achilles Tang territory, easily overwhelming the frantic defenders.

YELLOW TANGS * **lau'i-pala** (Zebrasoma flavescens), photo by D.R. Schrichte

Schools of **YELLOW TANGS** (Zebrasoma flavescens) flowing over the reef are a sight unique to Hawai'i. Although the species ranges as far as Japan and Guam, it is abundant only here. Along the calm Kona coast of the Big Island, Yellow Tangs often can be seen from shore, grazing on algae in the shallows. They are Hawai'i's most popular aquarium export.

SAILFIN TANG * **maneoneo** (Zebrasoma veliferum)

SAILFIN TANGS (Zebrasoma veliferum) are named for their remarkable dorsal and anal fins, which they suddenly extend when alarmed. By instantly appearing to double in size, they confuse predators.

INVERTEBRATES

MANY COLORFUL CREATURES LIVE ALONG THE ROCKY WALLS AND LEDGES OF THE LAVA SHORE. SEA SLUGS, SEA STARS, HERMIT CRABS AND OTHER ANIMALS CAN BE FOUND IN ABUNDANCE BY SHARP-EYED SNORKELERS AND DIVERS.

BLUE DRAGON SEA SLUG *(Pteraeolidia ianthina)*

The **BLUE DRAGON SEA SLUG** *(Pteraeolidia ianthina)* eats stinging hydroids. In an amazing biological feat, it incorporates the undischarged stinging cells of its prey into its own tissues, using them for its own defense.

The **WHITEBACK HERMIT CRAB** *(Ciliopagurus strigatus)* has striking orange-and-red banded legs and a chalk-white back. Its flattened carapace enables it to live in cone and miter shells that might not suit other hermit crabs.

WHITEBACK HERMIT CRAB *(Ciliopagurus strigatus)*

BLOODSPOTTED SEA STARS (*Linckia multifora*) are common along rocky shores, where they probably graze on algae. To reproduce, these stars can shed an arm, which then regenerates into a complete animal. Stars in the process of regenerating (with one long arm and four short ones) are called "comets."

BLOODSPOTTED SEA STARS (*Linckia multifora*)

FOUNTAIN SHRIMPS (*Stenopus pyrsonotus*) live in crevices, usually below 50 feet. This female carries a mass of light-blue eggs under her abdomen. She has lost a claw, which will grow back the next time she molts.

FOUNTAIN SHRIMP (*Stenopus pyrsonotus*)

GASKOIN'S COWRY * **leho** (*Cypraea gaskoini*)

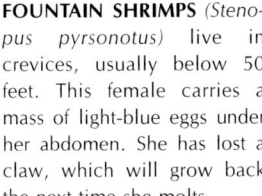

GASKOIN'S COWRY (*Cypraea gaskoini*) is found only in Hawai'i. The living animal's mantle is orange-red, covered with short, fleshy spikes. The bare shell (this one is occupied by a hermit crab) is equally pleasing. These cowries are found under ledges.

PREDATORS

THE ABUNDANT LIFE OF HAWAI'I'S ROCKY SHORES ATTRACTS ITS SHARE OF PREDATORS, LARGE AND SMALL, MOST OF WHICH ARE ACTIVE AT NIGHT. BEST KNOWN ARE THE SHARKS. EXCEPT FOR THE WHITETIP REEF SHARK, HOWEVER, THESE POWERFUL ANIMALS ARE RARELY SEEN. MOST COMMON ARE NUMEROUS SPECIES OF EELS, JACKS AND BARRACUDAS. NONE OF THE LATTER IS A THREAT TO RESPECTFUL HUMANS.

YELLOWMARGIN MORAY * **puhi** (Gymnothorax flavimarginatus)

The **SCARLET CLEANER SHRIMP** (Lysmata amboinensis) is doing the eating here, picking scraps from this **YELLOWMARGIN MORAY**'s teeth. The moray gets its name from the yellow margins of its tail tip. Large individuals attain about four feet.

WHITEMOUTH MORAY * **puhi** (Gymnothorax meleagris)

The **WHITEMOUTH MORAY** (Gymnothorax meleagris) attains a yard or more in length. The inside of its mouth is snow-white, easy to observe, because morays constantly open and close their mouths. People sometimes find this threatening, but it is just the eel's way of "breathing."

The **YELLOWHEAD MORAY** (Gymnothorax rueppelliae) prowls the reef by night, often completely emerging from its lair. Like most morays, it hunts primarily by smell.

The most vicious Hawaiian eel is the **UNDULATED MORAY** (Gymnothorax undulatus). Though it will not go out of its way to attack, it should not be trifled with. Divers and snorkelers who put their hands in holes are those most likely to be injured. It attains about three feet in length.

Growing to about five feet, the **VIPER MORAY** (Enchelynassa canina) is one of Hawai'i's largest and most potentially dangerous eels. Its hooked jaws (containing some of the longest, sharpest teeth in the moray family) meet at the tips only, giving the appearance of a perpetual snarl.

YELLOWHEAD MORAY * **puhi** (Gymnothorax rueppelliae)

VIPER MORAY * **puhi** (Enchelynassa canina)

UNDULATED MORAY * **puhi** (Gymnothorax undulatus)

HELLER'S BARRACUDAS * **kawele'a** (Sphyraena helleri)

Just offshore, glinting in the sunlight, silvery **HELLER'S BARRACUDAS** (Sphyraena helleri) slowly wheel and turn, waiting for dusk, when the hunting is best. (Among them, patient surgeonfishes wait for the remains of last night's meal.) These barracudas grow to about two feet in length.

A solitary **GREAT BARRACUDA** (Sphyraena barracuda) cruises the shoreline for its next meal. Large individuals attain almost six feet. They will not ordinarily attack humans. If the water is murky, however, glinting jewelry might be mistaken for the flashing scales of a silvery fish, with possibly unhappy results.

GREAT BARRACUDA * **kaku** (Sphyraena barracuda)

WHITETIP REEF SHARK * **mano la-la-kea** *(Triaenodon obesus)*

The **WHITETIP REEF SHARK** *(Triaenodon obesus)* is another common predator. A nocturnal hunter, it is adept at nabbing fishes and crustaceans from their hiding places in the coral. By day it usually rests under ledges or in caves. These sharks, which attain about six feet, are not dangerous to humans unless molested. Sharks of other species are rarely seen on Hawai'i's reefs.

MANTA RAY * **hahalua** *(Manta birostris)*, photo by David B. Fleetham

Giant **MANTA RAYS** *(Manta birostris)* feed on plankton and are predators only in the strictest sense of the word. A featured attraction along the Kona coast of the Big Island, they regularly approach shore to feed on small organisms attracted by hotel lights. Daytime sightings are infrequent. Large mantas attain a wingspan of 20 feet, although this size animal is rarely encountered.

CORAL REEFS

Coral reefs—the words conjure images of bright sun, clear water, undersea gardens, colorful fishes. For nature lovers with a taste for the sea, there is no greater paradise. Although modest compared to the coral ramparts of Micronesia, the South Pacific and the Caribbean, Hawai'i's reefs are just as enticing. They teem with beautiful fishes, turtles and fascinating invertebrate creatures. Many coral gardens in Hawai'i are accessible only by scuba, but snorkelers can view lush coral growth in shallow water along the Kona coast of the Big Island at Kealakekua Bay and Honaunau.

Reef scene, Kahe Point, O'ahu.

ANTLER CORAL (Pocillopora eydouxi)

SPECKLED SCORPIONFISH (Sebastapistes coniorta)

YELLOWSPOTTED CORAL GUARD CRAB (Trapezia flavopunctata)

ANTLER CORAL (Pocillopora eydouxi), Hawai'i's largest branching coral, serves as temporary or permanent shelter for many reef inhabitants. Nine fish species congregate in and around this big head off Molokini Island, Maui. Many smaller animals also dwell among its branches.

The **SPECKLED SCORPIONFISH** (Sebastapistes coniorta) spends its days wedged deep within branching coral, emerging at night to feed. Sometimes half a dozen or more occupy a single head.

The **YELLOWSPOTTED CORAL GUARD CRAB** (Trapezia flavomaculata) lives its entire adult existence deep within heads of branching coral, feeding on coral mucus and, perhaps, tissue.

LOBE CORAL *(Porites lobata)* is Hawai'i's most common coral, growing in both massive and encrusting forms from shallow water to beyond sport diving depths. Huge, mound-like colonies of Lobe Coral, such as this one at Honaunau, Hawai'i, occur in sheltered locations.

LOBE CORAL *(Porites lobata)*

Almost all the coral in this busy reef scene at Kealakekua Bay, Hawai'i, is Lobe Coral.

Reef scene at Kealakekua Bay, photo by Marcia Stone

Encrusting colonies of Lobe Coral are often home to **PETROGLYPH SHRIMPS** *(Alpheus deuteropus)*, which create and inhabit dark, branching channels reminiscent of ancient Hawaiian petroglyphs. The inch-long shrimps themselves are never seen.

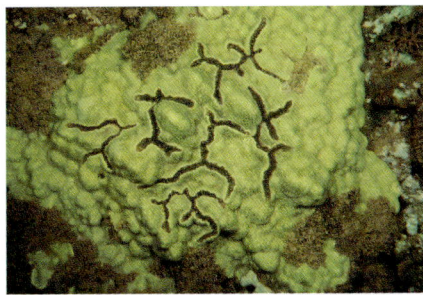

PETROGLYPH SHRIMP channels *(Alpheus deuteropus)*

A harem of female **PSYCHEDELIC WRASSES** *(Anampses chrysocephalus)* swim over Lobe Coral at Hanauma Bay, O'ahu. Their guardian male's splendid orange-and-blue head gives the species its common name. These wrasses occur only in Hawai'i.

PSYCHEDELIC WRASSE, male *(Anampses chrysocephalus)*

PSYCHEDELIC WRASSES, female *(Anampses chrysocephalus)*

YELLOW TANGS * **lau'i-pala** (Zebrasoma flavescens)

A pair of **YELLOW TANGS** (Zebrasoma flavescens) go their separate ways at Puako, Hawai'i.

CAULIFLOWER CORAL (Pocillopora meandrina)

CAULIFLOWER CORAL (Pocillopora meandrina) is abundant on hard lava rock from shallow water to moderate depths. This branching coral grows in small, rounded heads about a foot in diameter. The color ordinarily is brown but can be green or pink.

At Hanauma Bay, O'ahu, **PENNANT BUTTERFLYFISHES** (Heniochus diphreutes) school over a reef slope dominated by Cauliflower Coral.

PENNANT BUTTERFLYFISHES (Heniochus diphreutes)

SPOTTED EAGLE RAY * **hailepo** *(Aetobatus narinari)*

A **SPOTTED EAGLE RAY** *(Aetobatus narinari)* soars over a low reef of Cauliflower Coral at Kahe Point, Oʻahu.

Like the famous strangler fig of tropical forests, **PLATE CORAL** *(Porites rus)* specializes in overgrowing and smothering other reef corals. Here, it silently creeps over stands of Finger Coral at Honaunau, Hawaiʻi. This variable species, forming both plates and pillars, is common on the Kona coast of Hawaiʻi.

PLATE CORAL overgrowing Finger Coral, detail.

PLATE CORAL *(Porites rus)* at Honaunau, Hawaiʻi.

BLACKSIDE HAWKFISH * **pili-koʻa** (*Paracirrhites forsteri*)

A **BLACKSIDE HAWKFISH** (*Paracirrhites forsteri*) perches on Plate Coral at a depth of 90 feet below the Captain Cook Monument at Kealakekua Bay, Hawaiʻi.

COMMERSON'S FROGFISH (*Antennarius commersoni*)

On a colony of Plate Coral sits a baby **COMMERSON'S FROGFISH** (*Antennarius commersoni*). Looking like colorful sponges or algae-covered rocks, frogfishes are ambush predators. Barely able to swim, they wait patiently in one spot for small fishes or crustaceans to happen by, swallowing them faster than the human eye can follow. Although frogfishes are masters of camouflage, this inexperienced juvenile stands out boldly on the coral.

FINGER CORAL (*Porites compressa*)

FINGER CORAL (*Porites compressa*) is probably Hawaiʻi's second most common coral. It usually grows at depths of 30 feet or more and can form beds acres in extent. Much of Waikiki rests on a fossil reef composed of this species. Here, a Reef Lizardfish (*Synodus variegatus*) rests on Finger Coral at Honaunau, Hawaiʻi.

Large **FEATHER-DUSTER WORMS** (Sabellastarte sanctijosephi) frequently grow between branches of Finger Coral at Kane'ohe Bay, O'ahu. They instantly retract when touched.

Tracking its prey, an **ARC-EYE HAWKFISH** (Paracirrhites arcatus) perches on branches of Finger Coral, ready to pounce. Hanauma Bay, O'ahu.

In spaces at the bases of coral thickets live nocturnal crustaceans, such as this **BULLSEYE LOBSTER** (Enoplometopus holthuisi) and the colorful **HINGE BEAK SHRIMP** (Rhynchocinetes concolor). (Page 30-31)

Tiny **CORAL GOBIES** (Pleurosicya micheli) live on the surface of the coral, perhaps feeding on mucus and coral tissue.

FEATHER-DUSTER WORM (Sabellastarte sanctijosephi)

BULLSEYE LOBSTER (Enoplometopus holthuisi)

ARC-EYE HAWKFISH * **pili-ko'a**
(Paracirrhites arcatus)

CORAL GOBIES (Pleurosicya micheli)

BEDROOM COMMUNITY

MANY FISHES USE THE REEF ONLY AS SHELTER DURING THE DAY; AT NIGHT THEY FORAGE OVER NEARBY SAND. GOATFISHES AND SNAPPERS ARE TYPICAL OF THIS BEHAVIOR, RESTING IN ALMOST STATIONARY SCHOOLS DURING THE DAYLIGHT HOURS AND DISPERSING AT DUSK TO FEED. GOATFISHES ARE NAMED FOR THEIR BARBELS, REMINISCENT OF A GOAT'S BEARD, WITH WHICH THEY BUSILY "TASTE" THE SAND FOR WORMS, MOLLUSCS AND OTHER INVERTEBRATES. WHEN NOT FEEDING, THEY TUCK THE BARBELS UP OUT OF SIGHT. SNAPPERS ARE NOCTURNAL PREDATORS OF SMALL FISHES AND CRUSTACEANS.

YELLOWFIN GOATFISHES * **weke-`ula** *(Mulloidichthys vanicolensis)*

YELLOWFIN GOATFISHES (*Mulloidichthys vanicolensis*) hang out above a thicket of Finger Coral in Hanauma Bay, O'ahu. (Opposite page)

A group of **WHITESADDLE GOATFISHES** (*Parupeneus porphyreus*) bide their time on Lobe Coral at Honolua Bay, Maui. This species, known locally as **kumu**, is endemic to Hawai'i.

WHITESADDLE GOATFISHES * **kumu** (*Parupeneus porphyreus*)

BLUESTRIPE SNAPPERS (*Lutjanus kasmira*) are a showy species abundant on many reefs in Hawai'i. Introduced in 1958 for commercial purposes, they have undergone a population explosion, spreading all the way up the island chain to Midway. Unfortunately, they have displaced other more valuable native species while remaining something of a flop in island markets.

BLUESTRIPE SNAPPERS * **taape** (*Lutjanus kasmira*)

NURSERY

The intricate spaces between branches of Finger Coral make a perfect habitat for juvenile fishes, especially surgeonfishes. Here, a baby **CHEVRON TANG** (Ctenochaetus hawaiiensis) scrapes algae from a dead branch of coral. When it matures, it will turn almost entirely black and move up to the shallow, surge-swept rocky shore.

CHEVRON TANG (Ctenochaetus hawaiiensis), photo by Keoki Stender

Wafer-thin **YELLOW TANGS** (Zebrasoma flavescens), solitary when young, eventually move out of the coral to school in shallow water. Their color is so bright that they can often be seen from shore.

YELLOW TANG * **lau'i-pala** (Zebrasoma flavescens)

CORAL EATERS

CROWN-OF-THORNS SEA STAR (Acanthaster planci)

Many reef animals feed on living coral. Most browse lightly, doing no lasting damage. The **CROWN-OF-THORNS SEA STAR** (Acanthaster planci) is an exception. Notorious for its depredation of coral reefs, it everts its stomach over the living polyps, digesting them on the spot, leaving behind unsightly patches of white, dead coral. Up to 18 inches across, with 12 to 19 arms and covered with stout, sharp spines, it is an unusual star, more so because the sharp spines are venomous.

SPOTTED CORAL BLENNY * **pao'o kauila** (*Exallias brevis*)

The **SPOTTED CORAL BLENNY** (*Exallias brevis*) feeds exclusively on living coral, leaving little mouth marks ("blenny kisses") all over the reef. Densely covered with spots (reddish in males, brown to yellow in females), it raises a sail-like dorsal fin when alarmed.

ORNATE BUTTERFLYFISH * **kikakapu** (*Chaetodon ornatissimus*)

Among the world's most gorgeous fishes, the cream-and-white **ORNATE BUTTERFLYFISH** (*Chaetodon ornatissimus*) has black bars on the face and graceful orange lines along the body. It feeds only on live coral, readily entering shallow water at snorkeling beaches such as Hanauma Bay, O'ahu, to the delight of visitors and residents.

MULTIBAND BUTTERFLYFISH * **kikakapu** (*Chaetodon multicinctus*), photo by D.R. Schrichte

The **MULTIBAND BUTTERFLYFISH** (*Chaetodon multicinctus*) is another coral-eating species. Pairs follow each other closely over the reef, seldom lingering long in one spot and never overgrazing the coral. This butterflyfish occurs only in Hawai'i.

CORAL CRUNCHERS

Aptly named, parrotfishes are typically blue and green, with beaks heavy enough to crush rock. These large herbivores munch on living and dead coral to get at the algae living inside. Their scraping and crunching can easily be heard underwater. Gouge marks show where they have fed. Parrotfishes actually ingest coral rock, grinding it to fine sand with special bones in their throats. Organic matter is extracted and the sand expelled in a cloud through the anus. (The Hawaiian name for one species means "loose bowels.") It is said that much of the world's coral sand is produced by these fishes. Parrotfishes sometimes secrete a sleeping bag or cocoon of clear mucus at night, perhaps to ward off marauding moray eels, which hunt by smell.

SPECTACLED PARROTFISH * **uhu** (Chlorurus perspicillatus)

Close-up of SPECTACLED PARROTFISH

This big, blue-green **SPECTACLED PARROTFISH** (Chlorurus perspicillatus) is a Hawaiian endemic. It is a male; females are gray.

At Hanauma Bay, O'ahu, a female **BULLETHEAD PARROTFISH** (Chlorurus sordidus) sleeps soundly in her mucus cocoon.

BULLETHEAD PARROTFISH * **uhu** (Chlorurus sordidus)

REEF PREDATORS

BLUEFIN TREVALLY * 'omilu *(Caranx melampygus)*, photo by D.R. Schrichte

The **BLUEFIN TREVALLY** *(Caranx melampygus)*, known locally as Blue Ulua, is common on Hawai'i's reefs. Inshore, these predators hunt alone or in pairs; in deeper water, they may school by the hundreds. Hunting intensifies in the early morning or late afternoon, as schools of jacks flash swiftly by, making sudden changes in direction to confuse or isolate their prey.

GREEN LIONFISH and DWARF MORAY *(Dendrochirus barberi, Gymnothorax melatremus)*

Two small predators—a **GREEN LIONFISH** *(Dendrochirus barberi)* and a **DWARF MORAY** *(Gymnothorax melatremus)*—appraise each other on a reef off Makua, O'ahu. The lionfish, an ambusher of small fishes and crustaceans, may have second thoughts about this eel. The eel seems unconcerned. The two remained in this position for many minutes.

REEF LIZARDFISH * 'ulae, photo by D.R. Schrichte

A **REEF LIZARDFISH** (Synodus variegatus) displays a grinning mouthful of teeth as it waits for its next victim. Lizardfishes feed on other fishes.

The **TIGER MORAY** (Scuticaria tigrina) is a docile eel that has spots instead of stripes. When this eel was named, years ago, the word "tiger" meant any of the large cats, many of which are spotted.

TIGER MORAY * **puhi** (Scuticaria tigrina)

Groupers are large, bottom-dwelling predators common on coral reefs. Many are of commercial importance. Because Hawai'i lacks native shallow-water groupers, the Division of Fish and Game, in the 1950's, introduced three species from the South Pacific. Only the **PEACOCK GROUPER** or *roi* (Cephalopholis argus) has survived to reproduce. Juveniles, dark brown with iridescent blue spots, are especially beautiful.

PEACOCK GROUPER * **roi** (Cephalopholis argus)

SEA TURTLES

Hawai'i is one of the best places in the world to swim with turtles—they are abundant and protected by law. The GREEN TURTLE (Chelonia mydas) is most common, but Hawksbill Turtles Honu 'ea occur, as well. Early-morning snorkelers are likely to encounter turtles feeding at the edge of the reef or along the rocky shore. Later in the day they often rest in crevices or small caves. Algae grows abundantly on the turtles' backs. Sometimes they pause to be cleaned by surgeonfishes.

Turtles breathe air. Never "ride" a turtle or attempt to hold on to one—you could easily drown it. (Imagine someone five times your size trying to "ride" you as you come up for air.)

GREEN TURTLE * **honu** (Chelonia mydas)

GREEN TURTLE, detail.

GREEN TURTLE * **honu** *(Chelonia mydas)*, photo by D.R. Schrichte

A **GREEN TURTLE** cruises the reef.

Following page: GREEN TURTLE * **honu** *(Chelonia mydas)*
A **GREEN TURTLE** pauses over the reef to have its back cleaned of algae by Gold-Ring Surgeonfishes., photo by D.R. Schrichte

CAVES

WHAT IS MORE MYSTERIOUS THAN A CAVE? FOR SOME, CAVES ARE IRRESISTIBLE, FOR OTHERS FRIGHTENING. UNDERWATER, THEY ARE DOUBLY EXCITING (OR DREADFUL). LIKE CAVES ON LAND, SUBMARINE CAVES HOST A VARIETY OF CREATURES OFTEN FOUND NOWHERE ELSE. LUCKILY FOR DIVERS, MANY CAVE ANIMALS LIVE AT, OR NEAR, THE ENTRANCE. ALSO FORTUNATELY, MANY HAWAIIAN CAVES ARE ACTUALLY TUNNELS WITH TWO OR MORE ENTRANCES, MAKING THEM SOMEWHAT SAFER TO EXPLORE. IT GOES WITHOUT SAYING, HOWEVER, THAT NO ONE SHOULD PENETRATE DEEPLY INTO AN UNKNOWN UNDERWATER CAVE WITHOUT PROPER TRAINING AND EQUIPMENT. DIVERS DISTRUSTFUL OF CAVES CAN FIND MANY OF THE SAME ANIMALS UNDER THE LEDGES AND OVERHANGS ABUNDANT IN HAWAI'I'S UNDERSEA LANDSCAPE.

Sponges on cave wall

SPONGES

AMONG THE SIMPLEST OF ANIMALS, SPONGES ARE LIVING FILTERS WITH NO MOUTHS, STOMACHS, GILLS, HEARTS OR ANY OTHER ORGAN SYSTEMS. WATER IS DRAWN INTO THE SPONGE THROUGH TINY PORES. BACTERIA, PLANKTON AND OTHER ORGANIC MATTER ARE STRAINED OUT.

Communities of brightly colored sponges line the walls and ceilings of caves and the undersides of ledges, where there is little competition from light-loving corals and algae. Some sponges form irregular clumps; others, thin encrusting sheets. These bright assemblages grow in a submarine cave near the Lanai Lookout, O'ahu.

Sponges on cave wall

At O'ahu's Halona Blowhole, an underwater cave leads to the blowhole itself. A huge funnel, it channels the surge upward through tortuous crevices until it jets forth in a fountain of spray. Underwater, air compressed in the recesses of the cave explodes back causing shock waves—deep, powerful thuds that resonate in a diver's chest and make a depth gauge go wild. On the walls of this cave grow these branching sponge formations.

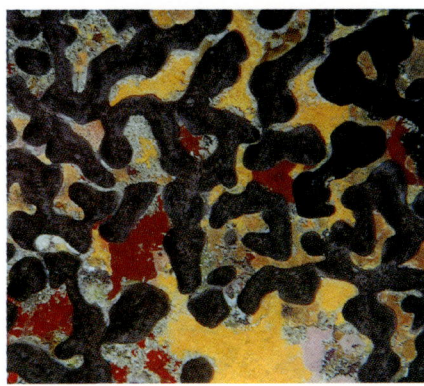
Sponges at blowhole cave

MOLLUSCS

MOLLUSCS ARE SOFT, LIMBLESS ANIMALS, WITH OR WITHOUT A SHELL. SNAILS AND SLUGS ARE MOST FAMILIAR, BUT OCTOPUSES AND SQUIDS ALSO BELONG TO THIS GROUP. THE MOST COMMON MOLLUSCS IN SUBMARINE CAVES ARE PROBABLY SEA SLUGS AND COWRIES, BOTH OF WHICH FEED ON SPONGES.

WHITEMARGIN SEA SLUGS *(Glossodoris rufomarginatus)*

WHITEMARGIN SEA SLUGS *(Glossodoris rufomarginatus)* attack a grayish-black sponge under a ledge near Pupukea, O'ahu. The white coils are their eggs.

SNOWBALL SEA SLUG *(Peltodoris fellowsi)*   Egg coil of the SNOWBALL SEA SLUG

The **SNOWBALL SEA SLUG** *(Peltodoris fellowsi)*, entirely white except for its black tentacles and gills, is found only in the Hawaiian Islands. Like most sea slugs, it lays a coiled ribbon of eggs, here photographed at the entrance to a cave off O'ahu's north shore.

GOLD LACE SEA SLUG *(Halgerda terramtuentis)*

The **GOLD LACE SEA SLUG** *(Halgerda terramtuentis)* reminds some people of a geodesic dome. The brown-and-white feathery organs are its gills. This slug occurs only in Hawai'i, often near the mouths of caves, but also under ledges on the reef.

LEVIATHAN COWRY * **leho** *(Cypraea leviathan)*

LEVIATHAN COWRY * **leho** *(Cypraea leviathan)*

The **LEVIATHAN COWRY** *(Cypraea leviathan)*, which occurs only in Hawai'i, frequently inhabits caves and probably feeds on sponges. By day the animal's mantle retracts, revealing the banded shell. At night the mantle extends to cover the shell, keeping it smooth and glossy. This cowry was photographed in a cave off the island of Lana'i called "First Cathedral."

ORNATE OCTOPUS * **he'e** *(Octopus ornatus)*

The **ORNATE OCTOPUS** *(Octopus ornatus)* comes out only at night. It is often seen in the vicinity of caves and ledges, where it probably hides during the day, here photographed at Makua, O'ahu.

HYDROIDS

Resembling delicate ferns, hydroids are colonial animals related to jellyfish, corals and sea anemones. Common in crevices and caves, they spread their tentacles to trap tiny planktonic animals drifting in the current. Powerful stinging cells quickly subdue their prey and also discourage predators. Hydroids can sting humans, causing burning that soon subsides, or itching that can last for days.

DIAPHANOUS HYDROIDS (*Sertularella diaphana*)

DIAPHANOUS HYDROIDS (*Sertularella diaphana*) sprout from the roof of a cave near the Lanai Lookout, O'ahu. Next to them grows a colony of **ORANGE CUP CORAL** (*Tubastraea coccinea*).

A **LONGNOSE BUTTERFLYFISH** (*Forcipiger longirostris*) probes with its long snout through feather-like colonies of stinging hydroids to pluck small organisms from the ceiling of a cave.

LONGNOSE BUTTERFLYFISH * **lau-wiliwili-nukunuku-'oi'oi** (*Forcipiger flavissimus*)

BLACK HYDROIDS *(Lytocarpia niger)*

Under a ledge off Lehua Rock, near the island of Ni'ihau, tangles of large, **BLACK HYDROIDS** (*Lytocarpia niger*) grow amid colorful sponges.

CORALS

FEW CORALS GROW IN CAVES OR UNDER LEDGES; MOST REQUIRE INTENSE LIGHT TO SURVIVE. CUP CORALS AND BLACK CORALS ARE AN EXCEPTION, LIVING ENTIRELY ON MINUTE PLANKTONIC ORGANISMS CAUGHT ON THEIR ORANGE, GOLD, GREENISH OR WHITE TENTACLES.

This beautifully extended polyp of **SOLITARY ORANGE CUP CORAL** (Balanophyllia sp.) was photographed off Hale'iwa, O'ahu.

COLONIAL ORANGE CUP CORALS (Tubastraea coccinea) are common on the undersides of ledges at Pupukea, O'ahu, where they sometimes grow amidst white **SNOWFLAKE CORAL** (Carijoa riisei), a soft coral that thrives in the same habitat.

SOLITARY ORANGE CUP CORAL (Balanophyllia sp.)

COLONIAL ORANGE CUP CORAL (Tubastraea coccinea) with SNOWFLAKE CORAL (Carijoa riisei)

BLACK CORAL *(Antipathes ulex)* with WINGED OYSTERS *(Pteria brunnea)*

In a cave deep beneath Lehua Rock, near the island of Ni'ihau, a bush of "white" **BLACK CORAL** *(Antipathes ulex)* grows near the entrance. Only the skeletons of these animals are black. Depending on the species, living polyps may be yellow, reddish or whitish. In this colony, **WINGED OYSTERS** *(Pteria brunnea)* grow in the branches.

HAWAIIAN LIONFISHES * **nohu pinao** *(Pterois sphex)*

Four **HAWAIIAN LIONFISHES** (*Pterois sphex*) congregate at the base of a "red" black coral tree growing under a deep ledge off Port Allen, Kaua'i.

The **LONGNOSE HAWKFISH** (*Oxycirrhites typus*) lives in and around bushes of "red" black coral, where its cross-hatch pattern makes excellent camouflage.

LONGNOSE HAWKFISH *(Oxycirrhites typus)*

Whip corals are solitary, wire-like relatives of black coral. They often harbor a pair of tiny **WHIP-CORAL GOBIES** (*Bryaninops yongei*), which spend their adult lives on the branch. At spawning time they clear a band of living tissue near the tip, where they lay their eggs. Here a goby guards its eggs under a deep submarine arch off Makua, O'ahu.

WHIP-CORAL GOBY *(Bryaninops yongei)*

CRABS

SLEEPY SPONGE CRAB * **makua-o-ka-lipoa** (Dromia dormia)

Using strong, sharp pincers, the slow-moving **SLEEPY SPONGE CRAB** (Dromia dormia) clips a piece of thick sponge from the roof of the cave to hold over its back. Thus camouflaged, it ventures forth at night to search for food on the nearby reef. Here, a pair of sponge-eating sea slugs go along for the ride. Good sponges are sometimes in short supply; in a pinch these crabs, up to eight inches across, will also carry old rubber slippers, bits of rope, or pieces of wood.

OPPOSITE PAGE:

The **RAINBOW SWIMMING CRAB** (Charybdis erythrodactyla) and the **HAIRY YELLOW HERMIT CRAB** (Aniculus maximus) are often seen on ledges near the roofs of caves. They are probably nocturnal, emerging from their shelter at night to feed.

RAINBOW SWIMMING CRAB *(Charybdis erythrodactyla)*

HAIRY YELLOW HERMIT CRAB * **unauna** *(Aniculus maximus)*

LOBSTERS

There are three kinds of lobsters in Hawai'i—spiny lobsters, slipper lobsters, and reef lobsters. Spiny lobsters crowd by day into cracks and crevices within caves. Strong, forward-pointing spines on their antennae and carapace protect them from frontal attack. Slipper lobsters have flat carapaces and rounded, shovel-like antennae. Only the small reef lobsters have claws.

The **BANDED SPINY LOBSTER** (*Panulirus marginatus*) occurs only in Hawai'i. Its tail is banded with white. The legs are dark purplish-blue, with faint stripes running lengthwise; the tail fan is bluish. Colorful knobs and spines adorn the carapace like jewels.

BANDED SPINY LOBSTER * **ula** (*Panulirus marginatus*)

BANDED SPINY LOBSTER ***ula** (*Panulirus marginatus*)

A baby **TRUMPETFISH** (*Aulostomus chinensis*) mimics a lobster leg in hopes of ambushing a small fish.

Banded Spiny Lobster with TRUMPETFISH

The **GREEN SPINY LOBSTER** (*Panulirus penicillatus*) is easily recognized by the conspicuous yellow-white stripes running lengthwise along its legs. The tail has no white bands; its outspread fan is almost solid green, edged with yellow or orange.

The **SCALY SLIPPER LOBSTER** (*Scyllarides squammosus*) often rests by day among cup corals on the roofs of caves.

GREEN SPINY LOBSTER * **ula** (*Panulirus penicillatus*)

SCALY SLIPPER LOBSTER * **ula-papapa** (*Scyllarides squammosus*)

REGAL SLIPPER LOBSTER * **ula-papapa** (Arctides regalis)

RED REEF LOBSTER (Enoplometopus occidentalis)

The **REGAL SLIPPER LOBSTER** (Arctides regalis) is beautifully adorned with reds, blues and yellows.

The **RED REEF LOBSTER** (Enoplometopus occidentalis), like many red animals, remains deep within caves by day, emerging only after dark, when its coloration makes it difficult to see. Stiff sensory hairs cover its claws and much of its body.

CAVE FISHES

TRUMPETFISH * **nunu** (Aulostomus chinensis) with SOLDIERFISHES * **'u'u** (Myripristis berndti)

A yellow **TRUMPETFISH** (Aulostomus chinensis) pauses by a crevice full of red **BIGSCALE SOLDIERFISHES** (Myripristis berndti). Although not true cave dwellers, trumpetfishes often hunt within caves. The soldierfishes are more typical of this environment, hiding in deep crevices by day and feeding over the reef at night. Because red light penetrates seawater poorly, red becomes equivalent to black after dark, making them hard to detect.

The **BIGEYE** (Heteropriacanthus cruentatus), another nocturnal fish, can be bright red, silver, or a blotchy mixture of the two.

BIGEYE * **'aweoweo** (Heteropriacanthus cruentatus)

BIGSCALE SOLDIERFISH * 'u'u *(Myripristis berndti)*

THOMPSON'S ANTHIAS *(Pseudanthias thompsoni)*

THOMPSON'S ANTHIAS *(Pseudanthias thompsoni)* are small, colorful, plankton-eating fishes related to groupers. They are often found near cave entrances in deeper water. Males, larger and more colorful, keep harems of females.

PORCUPINEFISH * **kokala** (Diodon hystrix)

The **PORCUPINEFISH** (Diodon hystrix) is a nocturnal feeder that rests in caves and under ledges during the day. If attacked, it inflates into a spiny sphere the size of a basketball—almost impossible to swallow.

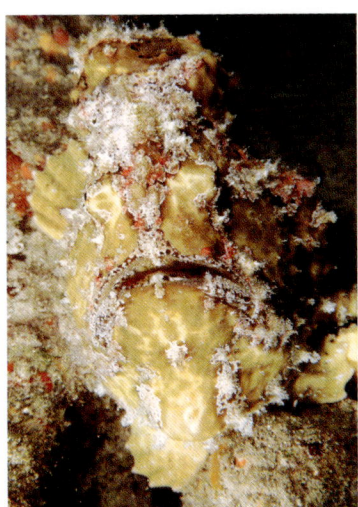

Compare this adult **COMMERSON'S FROGFISH** (Antennarius commersoni) with the smooth-skinned baby on page 28. Encrusted with scab-like patches and growths of different colors, it is barely recognizable as a fish. In a motion too fast to be followed by the eye, it can swallow prey almost as large as itself.

COMMERSON'S FROGFISH (Antennarius commersoni)

THE SAND

To many snorkelers and divers, the sand may seem a lifeless underwater desert. Nothing could be farther from the truth. Under and on this sea of sand live a host of intriguing creatures. Some spend quiet lives in tubes or holes, others actively plow their way through, or creep over, the ripples and dunes of its surface. Sand-dwelling fishes dive in and out, equally at home above the sand or under it. Here, predator and prey play out their lives with much the same intensity as on the more colorful reef. For those who take the time to explore it, the subtle world of the sand is equally as fascinating.

SAND PUFFER *(Torquigener florealis)*

The **SAND PUFFER** (*Torquigener florealis*) forages over open sand far from the reef. Sensing danger, it simply dives in, partially covering itself. This one kept its eye on the author for several minutes before finally disappearing entirely under the sand.

SAND PUFFER (*Torquigener florealis*)

GARDEN EELS (*Gorgasia hawaiiensis*) live by the thousands along deep, sandy slopes, stretching up out of their holes and facing into the current to feed on drifting plankton. When approached, they sink slowly back into the sand. Cautious, slow-moving divers, however, can enter a garden of waving eels, along a mysterious slope that beckons temptingly down into the blue abyss.

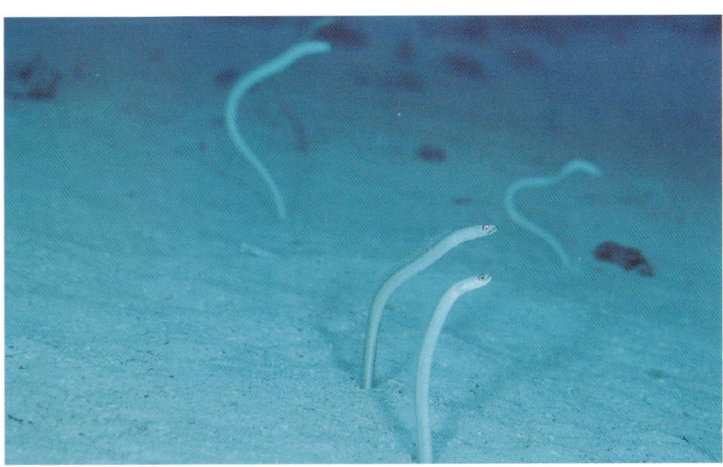

GARDEN EELS (*Gorgasia hawaiiensis*), photo by David B. Fleetham

AUGERS

Augers are marine snails with long, pointed shells reminiscent of the human tools of the same name. (Hawaiians used the shells as scrapers and stoppers for water gourds, as well as for drills.) They live just under the sandy surface, their slender, closely spiraled shells moving easily as the animals plow forward. Visible tracks on the surface allow divers and snorkelers to find them. Often in the five-to-six-inch range, the shells are quite attractive.

MARLINSPIKE AUGER * **pupu'ole** *(Terebra maculata)*

SPOTTED AUGER * **pupu'ole** *(Terebra guttata)*

CONES

THE CONES ARE THE LARGEST FAMILY OF MARINE SNAILS, MANY LIVING IN THE SAND ENVIRONMENT. THEIR SMOOTH, THICK-WALLED SHELLS, OFTEN BEAUTIFULLY PATTERNED, ARE ESPECIALLY POPULAR WITH COLLECTORS. ACTIVE AT NIGHT, THEY HUNT PRIMARILY BY SMELL AND STING THEIR PREY WITH A HOLLOW, VENOMOUS TOOTH OR BARB AT THE TIP OF A LONG PROBOSCIS. THEY CAN STING HUMANS, TOO—SOMETIMES FATALLY. IT'S BEST TO LEAVE THESE ANIMALS ALONE.

FLEA CONE *(Conus pulicarius)*

OAK CONE *(Conus quercinus)*

SEA CUCUMBERS

Lying like great sausages on the sand, **SEA CUCUMBERS** are a familiar sight to all snorkelers and divers. These headless, brainless creatures work their way slowly over the surface, ingesting quantities of sand at one end, extracting organic material, and dumping the processed remains at the other. Like the familiar sea stars and sea urchins, they belong to the large and important group of marine animals called echinoderms.

GOLDEN SEA CUCUMBER * **loli** (Bohadschia paradoxa)

These **GOLDEN SEA CUCUMBERS** (Bohadschia paradoxa) were photographed off the Kona coast of the Big Island.

GOLDEN SEA CUCUMBER * **loli** (Bohadschia paradoxa)

PARTRIDGE TUNS *(Tonna perdix)* are large, carnivorous snails. Their handsome, ribbed shells have a large opening from which extends a muscular foot of surprising size. (Fully extended, it appears much too large to fit back in.) This snail remains buried in the sand during the day, emerging at night to hunt sea cucumbers, which it immobilizes with an acid secretion. The sea cucumber sometimes escapes by detaching part of itself, which later grows back.

PARTRIDGE TUN * **pu'oni'oni'o** *(Tonna perdix)*

The **PANTHER FLOUNDER** *(Bothus pantherinus)* is a camouflage master of the sandy seabed. Its flat, oval body lies almost flush with the bottom. Virtually invisible to predator or prey, it waits patiently for the small crustaceans or fishes on which it feeds. Flounders and other flatfishes begin life with eyes on either side of the head. As they grow, one eye migrates over the top of the head, eventually joining the other on the opposite side. As this happens, the fish starts leaning over, eventually ending up flat on the sand with the blind side down.

PANTHER FLOUNDER * **paki'i** *(Bothus pantherinus)*

PANTHER FLOUNDER * **paki'i** *(Bothus pantherinus)*

KONA CRAB * **papa'i kua loa** (Ranina ranina)

KONA CRABS (Ranina ranina) are also called Frog Crabs. Squatting on their hind legs, they seem ready to spring. They never do. Like almost all sand-dwelling animals, they take refuge at the slightest hint of danger, digging their way backwards into the sand.

CLEARFIN LIZARDFISH * **'ulae** (Synodus dermatogenys)

The **CLEARFIN LIZARDFISH** (Synodus dermatogenys) sits motionless on the sand, blending in well. Propped on its pelvic fins, this ambush predator of other fishes tilts its head up for a better view. Just as often, however, it will wriggle into the sand, partially covering itself. In either case, powerful acceleration enables it to strike at fishes six or more feet away.

FLYING GURNARD * **loloa'u pinao** *(Dactyloptena orientalis)*, photo by Jerry Kane

The **FLYING GURNARD** *(Dactyloptena orientalis)* does not fly—it creeps along sandy bottoms using modified finger-like spines on its pelvic fins. When alarmed, it spreads its "wings" (an enormous pair of pectoral fins), greatly increasing its apparent size while simultaneously blending with the bottom. Ordinarily, the "wings" are kept folded along the side of the armored, box-like body.

PEACOCK RAZORFISH * **lae-nihi** *(Xyrichtys pavo)*

PEACOCK RAZORFISHES *(Xyrichtys pavo)* belong to the large, often colorful family of reef fishes known as wrasses. Although most wrasses are reef dwellers, the razorfishes have adapted to life in the sand by developing high, flat bodies with a wedge-like forehead. This enables them to dive in headfirst when frightened, and perhaps to "swim" short distances under the surface. Juveniles can be recognized by the long, stem-like dorsal filament projecting over their heads. Twisting and bending as they swim, they mimic drifting seaweed, the filament looking like a stem.

PEACOCK RAZORFISH, juvenile

MAGNIFICENT SEA STAR * **pe'a** (*Luidia magnifica*)

The **MAGNIFICENT SEA STAR** (*Luidia magnifica*) attains a diameter of at least two feet and is one of the most impressive Hawaiian sea creatures. This 10- or 11-armed giant lives just beneath the sand—its presence occasionally betrayed by a star-shape mark on the surface. If lifted out, it sinks slowly back in, digging busily with its thousands of large tube feet. It can also move with surprising speed over the surface. It is a voracious predator, feeding principally on other sand-dwelling animals.

HAWAIIAN SPINNER DOLPHINS (*Stenella longirostris*) have a distinctive three-toned color pattern not found on spinner dolphins in other parts of the world. Hunting and feeding at night, they rest and play close to shore by day, jumping in the air, spinning like a top, and falling back with a splash that is easily seen from land. Although dolphins are shy of divers, snorkelers can often get a good look at them as they frolic over the sandy bottom, here photographed at Makua, Oahu.

HAWAIIAN SPINNER DOLPHINS (*Stenella longirostris*), photo by D.R. Schrichte

COLORS

Hawai'i's reefs teem with colorful animals. What do they gain from their hues and patterns? Why do they stand out instead of safely blending in? Most often, bright colors are a warning, but each colorful species has its own story.

SPANISH DANCER *(Hexabranchus sanguineus)*

SEA SLUGS and FLATWORMS

"IN THE NATURAL WORLD," WRITES ZOOLOGIST EDWARD O. WILSON, "BEAUTIFUL USUALLY MEANS DEADLY. BEAUTIFUL PLUS A CASUAL DEMEANOR ALWAYS MEANS DEADLY." SLOW-MOVING SEA SLUGS AND FLATWORMS OFTEN FLAUNT VIBRANT COLORS AS THEY CREEP OVER THE REEF. FISHES TEMPTED BY THESE POISONOUS ANIMALS REMEMBER THE BRIGHT COLORS AND DO NOT REPEAT THE MISTAKE.

SPANISH DANCER *(Hexabranchus sanguineus)*

Up to a foot long, **SPANISH DANCERS** *(Hexabranchus sanguineus)* are among the largest, most conspicuous sea slugs in Hawai'i. They feed on toxic sponges, accumulating the poisons internally for their own defense. (opposite page) This one's head is in a crevice, probably consuming a sponge; the circle of feathery organs on the back are its gills.

(above) If touched, Spanish Dancers flare out their mantles in a colorful warning display.

The **VARICOSE PHYLLIDIA** (*Phyllidia varicosa*) is sometimes called the "scrambled egg slug." If molested, it secretes a substance distressing to fishes and crustaceans. These colorful animals should never be put in aquariums.

The color pattern and daytime habits of the **DIVIDED FLATWORM** (*Pseudoceros dimidiatus*) almost certainly mean that it is poisonous or distasteful.

VARICOSE PHYLLIDIA (*Phyllidia varicosa*)

DIVIDED FLATWORM (*Pseudoceros dimidiatus*)

REEF FISHES

Hawai'i's most colorful fishes share a similar lifestyle: they are the pickers and pluckers of the reef. Probing into cracks and crannies for small organisms and algae, snipping off bits of sponges or living coral, or picking small planktonic organisms from the water, they spend most of the day in the feeding mode. Many are territorial, and the classic explanation for bright "poster colors" in reef fishes has been that colors help fishes defend their turf. It is now thought that colors serve many other functions, as well.

MOORISH IDOLS * **kihikihi** *(Zanclus cornutus)*

If any fish stands out on the reef, it is the **MOORISH IDOL** (*Zanclus cornutus*). Gorgeous by anyone's standards, its light-gold body is banded with black in an almost-perfect blend of form and color. The orange-and-white snout and graceful trailing filament add an exotic touch. Although pleasing to humans, the conspicuous shape and color pattern may actually be a warning to predators. Moorish Idols feed on sponges—toxic to most other fishes. They probably taste awful.

ORANGESPINE UNICORNFISH * **umauma-lei** *(Naso lituratus)*

ORANGESPINE UNICORNFISH, caudal keels

The **ORANGESPINE UNICORNFISH** *(Naso lituratus)* has sweet orange lips and a Mona Lisa smile, but the base of its tail sports wicked orange spines that can shred an enemy's flanks—a splendid example of warning coloration.

ANGELFISHES

Quick-moving and shy, small angelfishes of the genus Centropyge usually live along the deeper slopes of the reef under ledges or in thickets of coral, where they are hard to spot. They seldom stay still for long—a flash of color revealing them as they dart from one hiding place to the next. Perhaps this is how they make themselves known to other angelfishes, either to attract mates or to warn away competitors of their own species. To predators, perhaps the color says, "I'm hard to catch and not worth the effort."

POTTER'S ANGELFISH (*Centropyge potteri*), rusty orange, black and blue, is common and a popular aquarium export. Living in small groups of a male and several females, it occurs only in the Hawaiian Islands.

POTTER'S ANGELFISH
(*Centropyge potteri*)

POTTER'S ANGELFISH (*Centropyge potteri*)

FLAME ANGELFISH *(Centropyge loriculus)*

The shy **FLAME ANGELFISH** *(Centropyge loriculus)*, a rare find in Hawai'i, is similar in its habits to Potter's Angelfish. Although it occurs as far west as Australia's Great Barrier Reef, specimens from Hawai'i are said to have a more intense color.

The **BANDIT ANGELFISH** *(Holacanthus arcuatus)* is white and gray with a bold black mask. Unlike other Hawaiian angelfishes, it is solitary, swims openly, and is easy to approach. Because it feeds on sponges, it probably tastes bad. Its unmistakable pattern is most likely a warning to predators, as well as an easy means of recognition for other lonely, roaming Bandit Angelfishes. The Bandit Angelfish occurs only in the Hawaiian Islands.

BANDIT ANGELFISH *(Holacanthus arcuatus)*

BUTTERFLYFISHES

What are the loveliest fishes? Many would say the butterflyfishes. Abundant everywhere along Hawai'i's shores, their disk-like bodies flash colors and patterns obviously meant to be noticed. As with terrestrial butterflies (which taste bad to predators), their colors may be a warning—butterflyfishes are spiny and make a prickly mouthful. The colors could also be for recognition—butterflyfishes travel in pairs and need to track each other on the busy reef. Yet another function may be the confusion of enemies. In some butterflyfishes a dark spot near the tail masquerades as the eye, the real eye being hidden by a dark bar. (The predator expects its prey to swim one way, and it swims the other.) Butterflyfish colors have even charmed human predators. In old Hawai'i, certain butterflyfishes, called kikakapu (meaning "strongly prohibited"), were considered sacred.

OVAL BUTTERFLYFISHES *(Chaetodon trifasciatus)*, photo by Keoki Stender

Coral-eating butterflyfishes are often very colorful. **ORNATE BUTTERFLYFISHES** (Chaetodon ornatissimus), **OVAL BUTTERFLYFISHES** (C. trifasciatus) and **FOURSPOT BUTTERFLYFISHES** (C. quadrimaculatus) may mate for life and almost always swim in pairs.

The **RACCOON BUTTERFLYFISH** (Chaetodon lunula) and the **TEARDROP BUTTERFLYFISH** (C. unimaculatus) both hide their eyes with a thick, dark bar. This is said to confuse predators.

OPPOSITE PAGE:
ORNATE BUTTERFLYFISHES * **kikakapu** (Chaetodon ornatissimus), photo by D.R. Schrichte

FOURSPOT BUTTERFLYFISH * **lau hau** (Chaetodon quadrimaculatus)

RACCOON BUTTERFLYFISH * **kikakapu** (Chaetodon lunula)

TEARDROP BUTTERFLYFISH * **kikakapu** (Chaetodon unimaculatus)

WRASSES

No account of colorful reef fishes would be complete without the wrasses. Males, females and juveniles often sport completely different outfits, their color patterns varying dramatically with age and sex. Until recently this confused even the scientists, who thought mama, papa, and junior to be entirely different species. What advantage wrasses gain by all these color changes is not completely understood. The fact that they can also change sex in mid-career does not simplify matters.

BELTED WRASSE, male * **'omaka** *(Stethojulis balteata)*

Male **BELTED WRASSES** *(Stethojulis balteata)* are green with vivid blue lines and a wide orange stripe. Their grayish-brown females are drab in comparison. The brighter color of males is doubtless for recognition. This species is endemic to Hawai'i.

Male **PENCIL WRASSES** *(Pseudojuloides cerasinus)*, like many species of wrasse, keep a "harem" of females. Females are cherry red, appearing grayish underwater at depth.

PENCIL WRASSE, male *(Pseudojuloides cerasinus)*

FLAME WRASSE, male *(Cirrhilabrus jordani)*

Scarlet and yellow male **FLAME WRASSES** *(Cirrhilabrus jordani)* are famous for their territorial and mating displays. Warning other males away from their territories (and their harems), they flare their fins and flash blue-white lines along their bodies. If a female strays too far, the male flares at her, bringing her back. Flame Wrasses occur only in the Hawaiian Islands.

FIVESTRIPE WRASSE (*Thalassoma quinquevittatum*)

The **FIVESTRIPE WRASSE** (*Thalassoma quinquevittatum*) and the **CHRISTMAS WRASSE** (*T. trilobatum*) both live in the surge zone of shallow reef flats. Their complex color patterns are similar.

RAINBOW WRASSES, juvenile * **hinalea** (*Coris gaimard*)

In **RAINBOW WRASSES** (*Coris gaimard*), color differentiates fishes by age rather than sex. Rainbow Wrasses undergo an amazing color change as they mature. Juveniles, red with white saddles, look nothing like adults with their brilliant blue spots and yellow tails.

RAINBOW WRASSE, sub-adult * **hinalea** (*Coris gaimard*)

The **HAWAIIAN CLEANER WRASSE** (Labroides phthirophagus) throbs with color, probably to attract customers. Mated pairs, identically patterned, inhabit a specific territory, such as a coral head, and make their living by picking parasites, dead tissue and mucus from the skin and gills of larger fishes. Other fishes will actually line up to be serviced by these busy little cleaners.

HAWAIIAN CLEANER WRASSE (Labroides phthirophagus)

CLEANER WRASSE and Ornate Butterflyfish

THE FOLLOWING PAGE:
CLEANER WRASSE and Whitemouth Moray, photo by D.R. Schrichte

CHRISTMAS WRASSE * 'awela (Thalassoma trilobatum)

PUFFERS and BOXFISHES

Slow-moving fishes with spotted color patterns are usually poor choices for predators. Boxfishes, sometimes called trunkfishes, are completely encased in a bony box—only their fins, eyes and mouths are movable. Pufferfishes can inflate into a tough, bristly ball that is too big to swallow. As a backup measure, both are poisonous. By using similar color patterns, these spotted fishes mutually enhance their chances of survival.

The male **SPOTTED BOXFISH** (Ostracion meleagris) is blue and black with white spots, trimmed with gold. The female is black, densely covered with white spots. When stressed, boxfishes secrete a poison from their skin.

SPOTTED BOXFISH, male * **moa** (Ostracion meleagris)

SPOTTED PUFFERFISH * 'o'opu-hue (Arothron meleagris), photo by D.R. Schrichte

The bristly skin of the **SPOTTED PUFFERFISH** (Arothron meleagris) has earned it the name Velcro Fish among divers.

The **HAWAIIAN WHITESPOTTED TOBY** (Canthigaster jactator) secretes an unpleasant-tasting substance from its skin when attacked, as well as inflating slightly. These little puffers occur only in the Hawaiian Islands.

HAWAIIAN WHITESPOTTED TOBY (Canthigaster jactator)

MORAY EELS

ZEBRA MORAY * **puhi** (*Gymnomuraena zebra*)

SNOWFLAKE MORAY * **puhi** (*Echidna nebulosa*)

Both the colorful **ZEBRA MORAY** (*Gymnomuraena zebra*) and the **SNOWFLAKE MORAY** (*Echidna nebulosa*) lack sharp teeth. One can only guess why these relatively harmless eels wear bright colors while their more dangerous cousins usually blend well with the reef.

FILEFISHES

Filefishes are so named because their rough skins, dried, were once used as files. When alarmed, they raise a stout dorsal spine. Many filefishes rely on camouflage for protection and are able to quickly alter their color to match the background.

SCRIBBLED FILEFISH ***loulu** (*Aluterus scriptus*)

The **SCRIBBLED FILEFISH** (*Aluterus scriptus*), whose tail is about one-third the length of its body, is normally covered with short blue lines, like scribblings. It can change color in a flash to blend with its surroundings.

SHY FILEFISH * 'o'ili (*Cantherhines verecundus*)

The **SHY FILEFISH** (*Cantherhines verecundus*) seldom strays far from cover. At the approach of the author, this one flattened itself against the rock, changed color and almost disappeared.

FANTAIL FILEFISH * 'o'ili-'uwi'uwi (*Pervagor spilosoma*)

The pretty **FANTAIL FILEFISH** (*Pervagor spilosoma*) spreads its orange tail in a mating or warning display. The spotted pattern hints that its thin, leathery body might not be good to eat. With few predators, it periodically multiplies out of control, washing up by the thousands on beaches. In old Hawai'i when this happened, they were dried and burned as fuel.

SCORPIONFISHES

SCORPIONFISHES ARE SLOW-MOVING OR SEDENTARY CARNIVORES, MANY WITH VENOMOUS SPINES THAT CAN DELIVER A PAINFUL STING. MOST ARE MASTERS OF CAMOUFLAGE ALMOST IMPOSSIBLE TO DETECT; A FEW, SUCH AS THE LIONFISHES, HAVE CONSPICUOUS COLORS AND ENLARGED FINS THAT ENHANCE VISIBILITY.

The **DEVIL SCORPIONFISH** (Scorpaenopsis diabolus) falls in the hard-to-detect category. It can match a variety of environments almost perfectly. If disturbed, it flashes brilliant yellows and reds on the underside of its pectoral fins to warn of venomous spines.

DEVIL SCORPIONFISH * **nohu** (Scorpaenopsis diabolus)

DEVIL SCORPIONFISH * **nohu** (Scorpaenopsis diabolus)

DEVIL SCORPIONFISH * **nohu**
(Scorpaenopsis diabolus)

DEVIL SCORPIONFISH * **nohu**
(Scorpaenopsis diabolus)

LEAF SCORPIONFISHES *(Taenianotus triacanthus)*

LEAF SCORPIONFISHES *(Taenianotus triacanthus)* come in solid or mottled colors—white, yellow, red, black and green. Thin like a leaf, they sometimes sway back and forth like a piece of seaweed. The author almost missed this pair, at Makua, O'ahu, due to their excellent camouflage. They are not venomous.

The **TITAN SCORPIONFISH** (*Scorpaenopsis cacopsis*) displays many colors on its mottled, tasseled exterior, becoming difficult to see against the background of the reef. The predominant reds help hide it at night, when it is most active. This species occurs only in Hawai'i.

TITAN SCORPIONFISH * **nohu** (*Scorpaenopsis cacopsis*)

The **HAWAIIAN LIONFISH** (*Pterois sphex*) is endemic to the Islands. The Hawaiians named them ***nohu pinao***, after the dragonfly. Their fanlike fins have a practical purpose—they help corner small fishes or crustaceans. For defense, the spines are highly venomous.

TITAN SCORPIONFISH * **nohu**, detail

HAWAIIAN LIONFISH * **nohu pinao** (*Pterois sphex*)

RED PENCIL URCHIN * **ha'uke'uke 'ula'ula** (Heterocentrotus mammillatus), photo by D.R. Schrichte

The **RED PENCIL URCHIN** (Heterocentrotus mammillatus) is common on Hawaiian reefs, seen here in a bed of soft Leather Coral (Sinularia sp.). Sharp-spined, dangerous urchins are usually black. The color of this harmless species makes it stand out vividly on the reef—to what advantage no one knows.